Food Truck Buyer's Guide

Buy, Build and Customize

Your Own Food Truck

By Andrew Moorehouse

A Free Gift for You

As a thank you for your purchase, here's a free resource for food truck entrepreneurs just starting out in this industry.

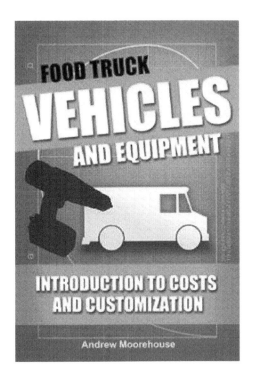

You'll get an introduction to food trucks and the vehicles used in the industry. In this booklet, you can find some basic costs of buying a food truck and learn about what food truck builders can do for you.

Visit the URL below for this exclusive offer:

TheFoodTruckStartup.com/free

Table of Contents

Introduction

Are you ready to learn about food trucks? I don't mean learning about the food truck industry... I'm talking about the wonderful mechanical vehicles themselves! I've come to realize that most people have very little information about the actual food truck vehicles that are in use today. So it prompted me to write this book that will hopefully shed some light on the vehicles and the systems that are incorporated into these mobile kitchens.

This is an exciting time to get into the food truck industry! I am constantly seeing new trucks on the road and hearing announcements of others throughout the country. If you are toying with the idea of starting your own food truck business, then keep reading!

This book will help you get a jump on your food truck education. I want to help prepare you as you start shopping for your own vehicle. I learned a lot myself researching the types of vehicles as well as what needs to go into them. You've seen the big delivery trucks in your neighborhood, right? Well, this book dives deep into how those delivery vehicles are transformed into food trucks. You'll also learn about choosing a builder as well as what needs to be installed in the kitchen area of the truck.

After you read this book, you'll have a new appreciation for the work that goes into each food truck. You'll probably also start noticing nuances each time a food truck or delivery vehicle drives past you. I know I can't stop examining those vehicles whenever I'm at a stop light now. I hope you find the information in this book enlightening and good luck with your entrepreneurial endeavors!

Andrew Moorehouse

Chapter 1: The Search Begins

The decision to become a gourmet food truck owner marks the beginning of an exciting step towards entrepreneurship. People from all kinds of backgrounds are attracted to the food truck industry because it is an area in the food and beverage industry that continues to grow in all major cities and has continued to expand to smaller cities and towns all around the country. Even some brick-and-mortar restaurants are embracing the idea of opening their own food trucks hoping to generate additional income and capitalize on the success gained from pioneers in this industry. Part of the success stems from the lower cost of entry into the market and the ability to have complete control over the unique styles of food that can be served up in these innovative mobile kitchens.

To join the ranks of the growing number of mobile food entrepreneurs, there has to be thorough planning in the startup stage as well as ongoing tweaks and adjustments to your business plan as you learn and grow. Many aspects of a food truck business need to be perfected and adjusted to get the right balance that works for your team as well as your customers.

Your menu, marketing plan, employees, cooking processes and ingredients are just some of the things that will need to flow smoothly in your business. Your food truck will essentially be the heart of your business because this is where customers will gather around and experience the tasty creations you have to offer!

Finding the right vehicle can be a long and stressful process. Most who start out often don't know what to expect or even where to look for a food truck. At this point, more questions than answers will arise. What types of equipment do I need? How does all that kitchen equipment get installed into the truck? What types of regulations do I have to follow? Who sells food trucks? You may not even have an idea of how much a food truck costs let alone getting one prepped for daily food service.

There are many factors to consider when you're in the market for a food service vehicle that will become the brand and physical presence of your mobile food business. It is also the key piece of equipment that allows you generate income as you prepare and sell delicious food to your customers. Buying a food truck is similar to buying a car on some aspects. It has to be reliable. It has to have a clean title. The vehicle must be in good working order and preferably have low mileage count.

Finding a truck in good mechanical condition is an important part of the buying process. Chances are, you've never had any experience with commercial vehicles and may not know what to watch out for. So it's a good idea to have a good mechanic on hand to check out the vehicle and prevent

surprises down the road. As with any purchase decision, it is helpful to arm yourself with some prior research on the vehicle you want to buy. That is what this book aims to do. The next section will give you some vehicle background and help you identify some of the various types of vehicles that can be used as food trucks.

Chapter 2: Introduction to Step Vans

Gourmet food trucks are primarily built on rectangular, box shaped vehicles called step vans. The term "step van" is commonly used as generic term today but it actually refers to the actual brand name of a commercial utility vehicle manufactured by Chevrolet. However, we will be using the generic term throughout the book. Up until now, you may not have known the technical name but step vans are most notably used as delivery vehicles by companies like FedEx and UPS. The commercial truck industry also refers to these vehicles as:

- Walk-in Delivery Trucks
- Bread Trucks
- Bakery Trucks
- Multi-Stop Trucks

These boxy step vans are ideal for food truck conversion because they offer convenient access to the entire interior including the cargo area without having to physically exit the vehicle. Users can freely walk from the front cab the driver seat to the rear of the vehicle easily. They also offer enough headroom so passengers can stand up in the cargo area. Step vans typically sit lower to the ground and have step wells that are also lower so passengers don't feel like they have to climb or jump out of the vehicle.

Step vans are available in standard lengths of 14 to 18 feet but can be up to 30 feet. Obviously the longer the length, the more difficult it will be to park and store. This can also be problematic when taking a longer vehicle to a mechanic for service or parking at a venue if they have limited parking space.

An important specification to understand is the measurement used to determine the length of the vehicle. The length specification actually refers to the interior cargo space and is measured from the back of the driver's seat to the rear wall of the vehicle. The indicated length is not the total length of the vehicle. For example, the total length of an 18 foot step van is approximately 29 feet from bumper to bumper. The 18 foot measurement refers to the interior cargo space in the back of the truck.

Step vans are constructed of two parts... the chassis and body. The chassis consists of a frame with front wheels, dual rear wheels, an engine and steering wheel. Currently, the two chassis manufacturers still in operation today are International and Freightliner.

However, since many step vans of the past are still bought and sold, you should become familiar with some of the other chassis brands. Common chassis manufacturers you might find on the new and used market include:

- Freightliner
- International
- Workhorse
- Chevy
- GM
- Ford

Most listings for step vans include the name of the chassis in their descriptions. This is good information to know when you're looking for parts or service.

Step Van Chassis and Body Manufacturers

International manufactures the P30042 and W52 chassis. The P30042 is a 16 foot chassis and the W52 is an 18 foot chassis. International chassis were formerly produced by Workhorse Custom Chassis which was formerly Cheverolet/GMC. Freightliner produces what they call the MT45 and MT55 step van chassis. Once these chassis are assembled, they are shipped to truck body builders to be transformed into finished vehicles. The body is built on and around the chassis and becomes an integral part of the whole vehicle. Because the body wraps around the chassis, the floor of the truck sits lower to the ground unlike box delivery trucks where the cargo box is mounted on top of the chassis.

The two primary step van body builders on the market today are Morgan/Olson and Utilimaster. Morgan/Olson was formerly Grumman Olson and their popularity is evident by the number of results that show up when searching online for used step vans. Here is a list of current and past body manufacturers you're sure to encounter in the commercial step van market:

- Grumman Olson
- Morgan/Olson
- Boyertown
- Utilimaster
- Supreme Body
- Union City Body
- Penn Body

Chevy/GMC Step Vans

One of the most popular step vans manufactured is the Chevrolet P30. Its popularity is obvious because the term P30 is also now used by many to reference step van vehicles in general. You will undoubtedly find many, many listings of P30 step vans in used vehicle searches. The P30 is available in 14, 16 and 18 foot lengths. Extremely popular is the 16 foot P30 because it is cost effective and has decent weight handling capability without being too large. The P30 also handles reasonably well on the streets. The 16 foot interior offers adequate space but whether it is the right fit for you depend on the equipment you will be installing.

Over the years, there have been several models of P30 with different weight capacities. This is measured in gross vehicle weight (GVW). The gross vehicle weight includes the vehicle itself plus any cargo and/or equipment on-board. From 1979 to mid-1980s, the P30 supported 10,000 pound GVW. This model was powered by a Chevy 5.7L 350 V8 engine with Turbo 400 transmission.

In later years, the P30 was upgraded to handle 14,000 and 16,000 pound GVW with the addition of heavier springs. P30s from the 1980s to 1990s were powered by 350 V8 and 454 V8 engines. Starting in 1982, Chevy introduced models with diesel engines which ranged from a 6.2L V8 to 6.5L V8. The diesel 6.5L engine became standard in models from 1994 and newer.

Between 1980 and 1993, Chevrolet also produced a heavier step van called the P60 (or CX-950) but it did not sell as well as the P30. However, the P60 can be found today as a rugged and reliable step van with great resale value. The GVW of the P60 is 23,000 pounds and is available in 18 to 24 foot lengths. Standard power plants include a 366 or 427 V8 gas or 8.2L diesel engines.

Freightliner Step Vans

The MT45 Freightliner step van comes in 16 or 18 foot models powered by either a Cummins or Mercedes engine. With a GVW of over 19,000 pounds, this vehicle could be classified as a medium-duty truck. The interior offers excellent square footage for food truck equipment and storage.

Freightliner offers another model called the MT55. It features a more power with either a 230 or 260 horsepower Cummins diesel engine and an automatic transmission. The MT55 comes in 18 to 26 foot lengths with a 23,000+ GVW. Both the MT45 and MT55 are excellent and reliable vehicles and convert extremely well to a food service vehicle.

Additional Makes and Models

The previous section focused on just a sampling of the most popular trucks manufactured and in use today. But they are not the only ones available. The following list consists of various makes and models of step vans that can be converted into a food truck.

Chevy P30
Chevy P42
Chevy Ultra Master

Ford E350
Ford E450
Ford F59
Ford P500
Ford P700
Ford P1200

Freightliner MT35
Freightliner MT45
Freightliner MT55
Freightliner M Line
Freightliner P500
Freightliner P700
Freightliner P1000

GMC P30
GMC P3500
GMC P42

International 1600
International FH1652

Oshkosh MT35

Workhorse P32
Workhorse P42
Workhorse P31842
Workhorse W42
Workhorse W50
Workhorse W62
Workhorse P500

Utilimaster 16 foot
Utilimaster 18 foot

This list will help you become familiar with the makes and
model numbers of the other step vans that food trucks are
built on. As you talk to sellers and do more research on

trucks, the list can be handy to have on-hand since these brands aren't really known as household names.

Step Van Rear Panel Modifications

Now that you know a little about step vans, you'll probably notice that a large number of them have sliding rear doors on the back that raise up like a garage door. This is ideal for delivery vehicles but not necessarily for food trucks. The reason is that slide up doors eat up space on the interior of the truck. It reduces the amount of headroom in the cargo area and can be a problem for tall passengers working in the kitchen area. And because the sliding door is exposed to the elements, it can cause a problem of dropping dirt and debris into your kitchen area and your food.

If the truck you are considering to buy has a sliding rear door, chances are that it will have to be replaced by swinging doors attached by hinges. The installation of swinging doors allows full clearance of the cargo area right up to the ceiling. Food truck builders are fully capable of this type of modification.

There are some instances where no doors are needed on the back of the vehicle. This means the rear panel of the truck will be replaced by a wall. This type of modification will be needed if your cooking equipment is mounted to the rear of the vehicle where a doorway is not necessary. Additional venting to the exterior may be part of this rear wall if griddles, stoves or other cooking equipment are mounted in this area.

Additional Information on GVW

As mentioned earlier, the gross vehicle weight is the total weight capacity of the truck. This includes the weight of the truck itself, cargo, equipment, driver, fluids, fuel and anything else that goes in the vehicle. The vehicle must not be overloaded past its GVW specifications. Step vans are placed into different classifications depending on GVW.

Class 4 - 14,000 to 16,000 GVW
Class 5 - 16,001 to 19,500 GVW
Class 6 - 19,501 to 26,000 GVW
Class 7 - 26,001 to 33,000 GVW

Class 7 vehicles require a commercial driver's license (CDL) and additional licensing standards. Most food trucks used for food trucks fall below the 26,000 pound GVW which allows operation with just a standard Class C driver's license. However, if your truck and equipment hovers close to your GVW, be sure not to overload the truck to stay within legal operating limits.

Trailers with GVW of 10,001 may require a CDL if the combined weight of the trailer and vehicle towing the trailer is 26,001 pounds or more. Some people might overlook the fact that trailer requirements take the combined weight of both the motorized vehicle and the trailer itself.

Chapter 3: Where to Find Food Trucks for Sale

When you start your search for a vehicle, the first question that often comes to mind is where to find food trucks or step vans on sale? Obviously the quickest and most convenient place to start is locally in your own town. Get to know some of the other food truck owners in your area and ask them where they found their truck. Food truck owners are usually happy to answer questions like this however they might be a little hesitant if the food truck you are going to operate competes directly with theirs. But in any case, getting the information straight from people who have already gone through the process is a great place to start.

You can also call or visit local commercial vehicle dealerships to see what type of inventory they have on hand. In some cases, these dealerships are part of a bigger automotive network and can search their inventory in other regions where they do business. The advantage of going to a commercial vehicle dealership is that you can evaluate the vehicle immediately.

Keep in mind that used inventory can be sparse. Often, you'll find that dealer inventory consists of used trucks that were

delivery vehicles or other sorts of commercial utility vehicles that are not suitable for food trucks. But if you're fortunate enough to find a truck that has been previously converted to a food service vehicle, the time it takes for you to get it ready and operational can be dramatically minimized.

Of course, online options are plentiful when it comes to searching for a food truck. And chances are you will be able to find a fully equipped food service vehicle online. Whether it's located near you is another story. Starting your search on your city's Craigslist site gives you the best chance of finding a vehicle locally. Often, you'll find private sellers that either are going out of business or who are selling their business to move onto other endeavors. You can sometimes find the best deals this way if the owners need to sell quickly.

Searching Nationwide

If you can't find any local vehicles that fit your needs, then you'll have to expand your search on websites that have listings for a wider region or even the whole country. The choices are definitely better but the disadvantage is that the vehicles are located further away and you can't easily evaluate them in person. Here are some of the commercial vehicle sites where you can do additional research and find available vehicles from around the country:

- CommercialTruckTrader.com
- TruckPaper.com

- TruckerToTrucker.com
- UsedVending.com

eBay is also a great place to conduct your research. You can find vehicles from both private and commercial sellers as well as get a good idea of pricing for vehicles in different conditions and with different options. There are also fully equipped trucks as well as base vehicles that need to be converted to a food truck.

With any of the online options, you the buyer will be responsible for all shipping and delivery charges unless you travel and drive the truck back to your hometown yourself. Be sure you are familiar with driving a commercial vehicle and verify whether you'll need a commercial driver's license or not before you take the vehicle on the road.

Chapter 4: How Much Does a Food Truck Cost?

Your budget is the primary limitation when it comes to shopping for a food truck. It will most-likely be your biggest single expense when it comes to starting your mobile food business. As with any vehicle purchase, the number of features and options will determine the price. A fully equipped truck is going to be more expensive but it will save you time if you're trying to get operational sooner. You also have the option of buying new or used which also plays into the final price of the truck.

You may be able to save a little money by purchasing a base vehicle that can be converted into a food truck. But depending on the complexity of the remodel and the type of equipment you install, you could pay just as much as a fully equipped used vehicle when the build is completed. Please keep in mind that the dollar figures mentioned in this section are only estimates because every vehicle is going to be different depending on the build.

The most expensive option is to buy brand new from a truck builder. When buying new, you have the advantage of receiving pristine equipment and warranties that come from a new vehicle purchase. You also have the option of having the kitchen built exactly to your specifications and needs.

A brand new custom food truck can cost you $100,000 or more but you get to start fresh with everything in working order and the pride of owning a brand new vehicle. That $100,000 figure can go up or down depending on the size of the truck and how much equipment you'll need installed. Custom truck builders often bundle in other services like kitchen design, equipment options, graphics design and vehicle wraps together.

Custom Truck Builders

Custom builders can also construct food trailers for those who would rather go with a trailer instead of a traditional food truck. New food trailers can range in price from $15,000 to $30,000. Obviously the price difference is quite dramatic but with a food trailer, you must employ a second vehicle to tow it around. For many mobile food business owners, using a food trailer is a great way to get into the business at a lower cost. But having to tow it around is not something every potential owner is prepared to deal with.

For those who are trying to keep tight startup budgets in check, the most popular option is to buy used vehicles and trailers. Used vehicles and trailers can come fully equipped or as a base unit that needs customization. It is possible to find a used vehicle that comes complete with all the pieces of equipment you will need to run your business without

needing modifications. But if there are changes that need to be made, it takes far less time to make small modifications to a unit that has already been built into a food service vehicle.

Fully-equipped used food trucks can be priced from $25,000 on the low end to $80,000 or more on the high end. The price depends on the condition, year and the type of equipment that has already been installed. Used concessions trailers can range from $3500 to $15,000. This price includes fully equipped kitchens.

If you start with a used base vehicle (which is practically an empty truck), the price can start at $10,000 and go up to $35,000+ without any kitchen equipment. You will then have to factor in the cost of the conversion to a food service vehicle. You can take your basic vehicle to a custom truck builder where they can help design and implement the necessary equipment to convert the vehicle into a fully functioning food service vehicle. With this option, you get a used vehicle but you have the advantage of a brand new kitchen and equipment to cook with.

Chapter 5: What to Expect from a Custom Food Truck Builder

Custom food truck builders can be found in many major cities. However, their clients can be local or national which help expand your options when it comes to finding a builder for your project. Some of these companies ship custom food trucks to international locations as well.

Food truck builders usually offer full-service concept and design services for food truck owners. These builders job is to offer their expertise to help you design the perfect catering trailer or truck. They are also knowledgeable in building vehicles that adhere to strict safety regulations. When employing a custom truck builder, you need to check out their previous projects and even talk to the owners of the trucks/trailers they've built to see if their customers are satisfied with the results.

Truck builders should be knowledgeable in safety and fire suppression systems as well as servicing electrical wiring and connections. They should also be familiar with the various types of mobile kitchen equipment as well as proper installation into a vehicle. Most custom truck builders should be able to take your project from start to finish depending on the services they offer. This is what you want to find because it's much easier to deal with one contact or company that can coordinate each phase of your vehicle build. This includes:

- Concept Planning and Design
- Electrical Systems
- Fire Systems
- Custom Detailing Services
- Graphic Design
- Plumbing
- Vehicle Wrap Installation
- Equipment Sales and Installation
- And More

If you are working with an out-of-state builder, confirm that they are familiar with the health codes and safety regulations for your city or state. Check to see if they've built vehicles that are operating in your state. In many cases, you may have to provide the specific rules and information to your builder.

Completion times can vary widely between different builders with some stating that they can finish builds in as little as 2 weeks. However, you should always expect delays and extended build times. These delays can come in many forms including equipment permits, inspection scheduling, safety violations, equipment availability and more.

During the planning and building stage, it's a good idea to imagine being inside the truck preparing meals to identify

where the bottlenecks might occur. Arrange to personally inspect and evaluate the interior during the build phase. Every piece of equipment you put into your truck takes up valuable space. The last thing you want is realizing that you placed a grill or cooler unit in the wrong spot after your truck or trailer has been delivered to you.

Vehicle Wrap and Exterior Design

It's actually astonishing how much money can be spent building the interior of your food truck. Installing the necessary equipment with an efficient layout is a major part of a step van conversion. However, the exterior of your vehicle requires just as much thought and planning. With your mobile food business, you only get one chance to create a great first impression... This happens long before a customer has even ordered food from your truck. Within the first few seconds of seeing your food truck, potential customers will immediately make decisions of whether or not they will order food from you. They may buy from you at that moment or their first visit could come days or weeks later because they remembered your truck design.

Your vehicle wrap alone can single-handedly convey the overall tone and style of your mobile food business to your customers. Marketing experts have shown that vehicle wraps are noticed and remembered better in almost all types of advertising except for TV ads. In terms of expenses, designing and wrapping can cost somewhere between $3,000 and $5,000.

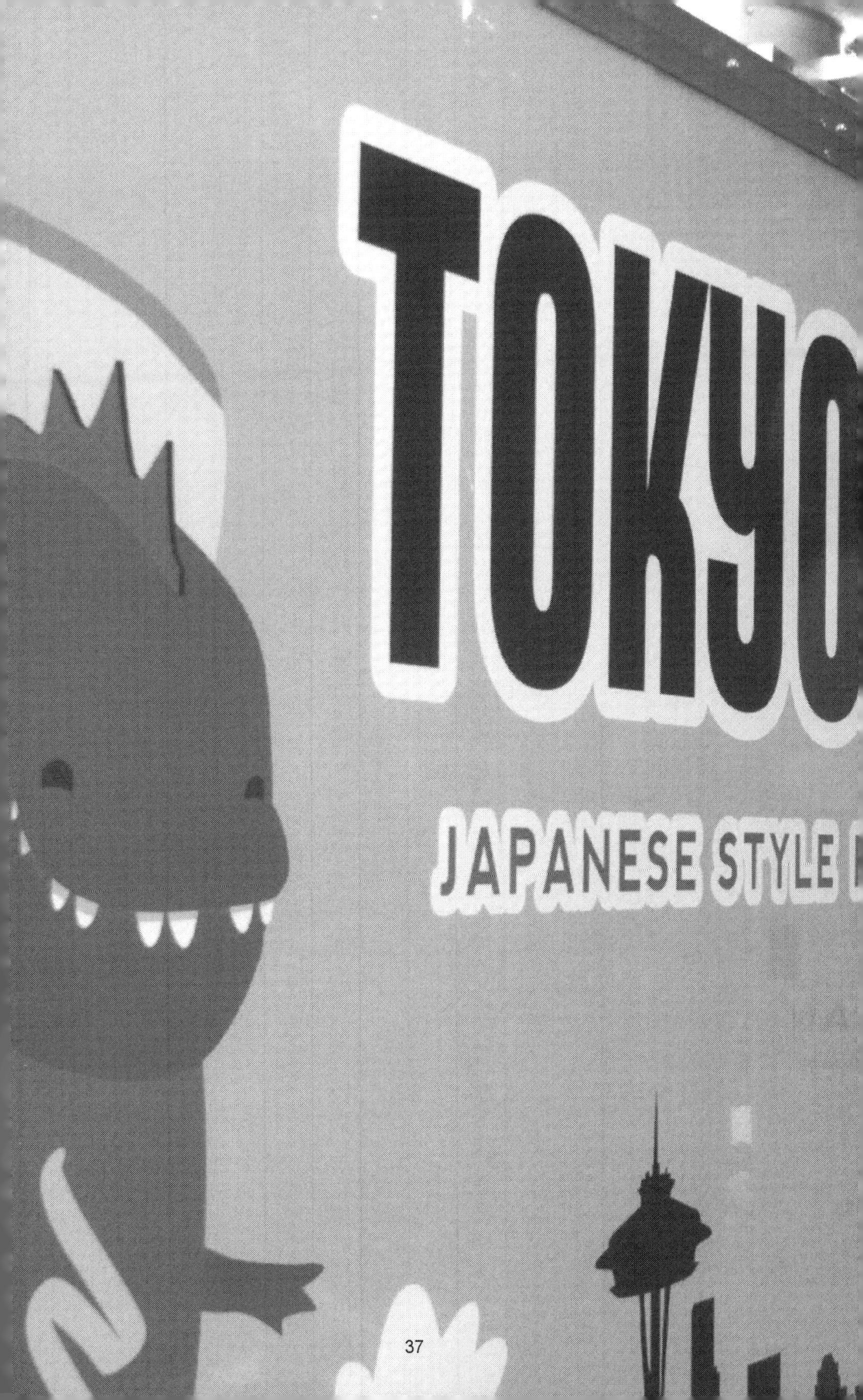
TOKYO
JAPANESE STYLE

Your graphics should be bright and easy to read. The goal is to help bring attention to your truck and hopefully attract more customers. The vehicle wrap literally turns your vehicle into a mobile billboard that can express the atmosphere around your truck and give a sense of the type of food you serve as well as your contact information. Your wrap is one of the most important components in your brand. The graphics on your wrap can then be incorporated to other elements of your marketing materials. This includes graphics for your website and packaging like cups, napkins, business cards and more. According to some, one of the downsides of vehicle wraps is that the adhesives that are used on the vinyl panels only last about 5 years when exposed to the outdoor elements. However, that time frame is just an estimate and your wrap could stay intact much longer. If you operate in a metropolitan area with lots of high buildings, consider extending your wrap to the roof so that people looking down on the street can recognize your truck.

Regarding contact information on your vehicle wrap, be sure to also include your website address, Facebook and Twitter tags on the sides and back panels of your food truck. The exterior without a doubt is the most visible part of your business so it's worth including your company details on the side. Keep your contact information large enough to be readable from a moderate distance but don't let it distract customers from your main logo and brand graphics.

If you want to save money on your exterior graphics, you don't have to wrap the entire vehicle. You can instead have just your logos printed on large vinyl sheets that act like giant

stickers that your installer can adhere to the sides of your vehicle. If you want to coordinate the base color of your vehicle with your logo, consider having the exterior of your truck painted a single color before adding your vinyl logos and contact information.

Chapter 6: Driver's License Requirements and Insurance

One overlooked detail when starting a food truck business is the type of license a driver needs to legally drive a food truck. This will depend on the gross weight of the vehicle. This figure is the total weight capacity of a fully loaded vehicle. It includes fuel, passengers, accessories, cargo and equipment. Depending on the truck you plan to use, a standard driver's license will allow you to drive a vehicle up to 26,000 GVW. That's reassuring because most food trucks can weigh between 8,000 and 16,000 GVW.

If you do end up owning a vehicle with a GVW of 26,001 or more pounds, a commercial driver's license or CDL is necessary. Usually a Class B driver's license will be required in this type of situation. The license requirements mentioned here are just simplified explanations but you will need to check with your city or state to learn more about the specific requirements to avoid any possible fines and issues related to driving with the wrong type of license.

Food Truck Insurance

We need to preface this section with the following disclaimer: We *are not* insurance agents and none of this information should be considered official legal advice. You should consult with an insurance professional when it comes to insuring your business and protecting your assets.

While you may well be on your way to building a great food truck, there's one more part of the equation that needs to be addressed when it comes to your vehicle and business. That's where insurance comes in. Whenever customers do business with you, there's always the risk that something could go wrong. Common incidents like bodily injury or property damage can happen at any time and you need to be protected from expenses and claims that could arise suddenly.

Nobody knows when an accident will happen but even small claims could put your business in a dire situation. Claims can also come from your employees from accidents that happen on the job. But you need to realize that accidents don't just happen in the kitchen. Simply driving your truck from one location to another opens up many possibilities for accidents from you or other drivers on the road. And don't forget that your truck can even be stolen which could put you out of commission for days/weeks or be completely devastating for your business.

When shopping for insurance for your food truck, make sure the insurance company understands the needs of mobile food trucks and their owners. The food truck industry is just a small segment of the food and beverage industry and you need to be sure the provider you choose can offer the coverage you need. Some of the services you should ask about are:

- General Liability
- Commercial Auto Liability
- Operations Coverage
- Products Coverage
- Damage to Premises
- Personal Property Coverage
- Business Property Coverage
- Cyber Liability Insurance
- Workers' Compensation
- Unemployment Insurance
- Umbrella Coverage (Excess Liability)

The insurance companies will also perform checks on the persons who will be driving the food truck. These come in the form of Motor Vehicle Reports. Drivers you employ who fall into a particular risk profile will result in higher premiums for your business. It's possible that the insurance provider may choose not to cover your business at all because of risky drivers on your payroll. So before you apply for insurance, check the driving records of your drivers to see how many moving violations or accidents (if any) they've had in the last 36 months.

Additional Insurance Requirements

If you plan on doing business at various venues and events, you may need to prove that you are insured before you are even allowed on the property. This is typically called an Additional Insured Certificate. This can include venues like food truck pods, festivals, private locations and more. Most venues require that your policy includes at least $1 million General Liability coverage. This protects the venue or event from accidents caused by your business activities on their premises. Each certificate can cost $25 to $100 or more. If you attend many events during a year, these expenses can add up quickly. But definitely ask up front whether an insurance provider requires fees for these certificates. There are some insurance companies that won't charge you extra for this service.

Do your research in this area and get advice from an insurance professional. Since food trucks consist of only a small portion of the food and beverage industry, some insurance companies may not be familiar with the specific policies or requirements for food trucks. Make sure you ask a lot of questions and find out if they are familiar with the food truck industry and the needs of food truck owners. Similar to consulting with a medical doctor, it's worth getting second and third opinions on this subject to make sure you're protected!

Chapter 7: Additional Equipment Costs

When starting your research, it can be difficult to find information to help you calculate the cost of building a food truck. In this section, you'll find different types of equipment with approximate costs to help you get a better idea of the startup costs as it relates to equipping your food truck. The approximate costs listed below are in USD:

Vehicle Systems

- Water System: $4200.00
- Propane System: $4000.00
- Exhaust Hood: $3500.00
- Generator Compartment: $1200.00
- Fire Suppression System: $3200.00
- Interior Sliding Window: $700.00

- 19 cu. ft. Refrigerator/Freezer: $750.00
- Small Freezer: $430.00
- 27" Sandwich Fridge: $2400.00
- 48" Sandwich Fridge: $3400.00

- 60" Sandwich Fridge: $3700.00
- Single Door Cooler: $1400.00
- Double Door Cooler: $2600.00

- Full Size Steamer/Warmer: $1400.00
- Double Steamer/Warmer: $2800.00
- Triple Steamer/Warmer: $4200.00

- 24" Range: $4100.00
- 36" Range: $4600.00
- 2 Burner Stove Top: $1100.00
- 4 Burner Stove Top: $1800.00
- 6 Burner Stove Top: $4000.00

- 18" Griddle: $1600.00
- 24" Griddle: $2300.00
- 36" Griddle: $2800.00
- 48" Griddle: $3200.00

- 18" Char Broiler: $1700.00
- 24" Char Broiler: $2100.00
- 36" Char Broiler: $2700.00
- 48" Char Broiler: $3000.00

- Wall Mounted Potato Cutter: $380.00
- Double Crepe Griddles: $2200.00
- Gyro Machine: $2800.00
- 40lb Two Basket Deep Fryer: $1900.00
- Pizza Oven: $6000.00

As you can see, your costs can add up pretty fast even with just minimal cooking equipment on board your truck. The approximate prices listed above are for new items only. But you can find good deals on used equipment from websites like eBay or Craigslist.

Chapter 8: Power Generators and Propane

When you're out on the streets, your truck needs to be self-sufficient. Every piece of equipment needs to be able to run on its own without a tether to hard-line power sources and gas resources. This is accomplished with propane tanks and electrical generators. Every food truck needs both to be able to operate unless you are at a food truck park or other venue with available shore power and gas hook-ups.

Portable generators supply the electricity to your on-board appliances which includes refrigerators, toasters, waffle irons, blenders, payment systems and more. Some trucks have compartments designed for specifically to house power generators and keep them out of sight and to reduce noise. Food trucks that do not built-in enclosures will have power generators placed next to their trucks with power lines connected through ports on the side of the vehicle.

Determining the size of generator (wattage) you need depends on the equipment you have on-board. The best way to do this is simply to take inventory of all the electrical appliances you will be using. Then add up the wattage or amperes (amps) required by all of your appliances. You'll also

need to know which appliances you'll be using simultaneously to avoid overloading your generator during your preparation and food service.

Total wattage in an appliance is calculated using this equation:

Watts = Amps x Volts

For example, if your device is rated at 5 amps and 120 volts, the wattage requirements of that device is 600 watts (5A x 120V = 120 Watts).

Sudden Power Surges

After you've made your calculations, add up the total wattage to help you choose the right generator for your truck. To avoid potential shut-downs, you will need to anticipate some extra available wattage use when choosing a generator. Some appliances will draw more power on startup or at different intervals so you will need extra capacity for that. Fortunately, most generators have a surge or peak power rating. The peak power rating indicates the amount of additional wattage the generator can produce for very short periods of time.

A sudden draw of power may happen when you start any electrical appliance. For example, a refrigerator may require 2200 watts to start its compressor (starting wattage) and then 700 watts to run after that (running wattage). When you add up your wattage requirements, you need to use the starting wattage in your calculations.

It's a fact that running a generator creates a lot of noise not to mention the exhaust fumes. Most food truck owners will place their generators on the opposite side of their vehicle away from the service window to keep noise to a minimum for their customers. Some food truck owners may even use two generators at the same time. But be aware that you will need to haul these heavy machines in and out of your truck each time you use them unless they're mounted in a compartment on your vehicle.

Propane Tanks

While it is vital that you know the electrical requirements of your appliances, you will also need to be able to anticipate the amount of propane you will need for your truck so you won't run out at the busiest time! Propane tanks have approximate BTU ratings that you will use along with the BTU ratings of your gas appliances to help determine how long a propane tank will supply gas to your truck. The BTU ratings on an appliance assume that you will be operating the appliance at 100%. For example, the calculations are made on gas grills with all burners set on high or a water heater set at the maximum temperature.

If you don't know the size of your tank, the first thing you need to do is measure the height and diameter of your propane tank. Do not include the height of the collar at the bottom (and top) of the tank. The collar is just used as a base to keep the tank upright. The diameter is measured at the widest point of the tank. Here are some common tank sizes to help determine the capacity of a new or existing tank:

20lb tank = 18 inches high x 12.5 inch diameter
30lb tank = 24 inches high x 12.5 inch diameter
40lb tank = 29 inches high x 12.5 inch diameter
100lb tank = 48 inches high x 14.5 inch diameter

Once you know the tank size, you can then determine the BTU capacity when it is full. The following list displays the BTU capacity of the various tank sizes:

20lb tank = 430,270 BTU
30lb tank = 649,980 BTU
40lb tank = 860,542 BTU
100lb tank = 2,160,509 BTU

Next, you need to find all the BTU ratings of your propane powered equipment. You can usually find the BTU rating stamped or printed on the appliance itself. If you can't find the rating on the appliance, you will have to consult the owner's manual or contact the manufacturer. If you purchase new equipment, it's a good idea to keep all your manuals in a safe place for future reference.

After you have added up the BTU ratings of your gas appliances, divide this number with your propane tank BTU number to calculate the number of hours your propane tank will be able to supply fuel to your appliances at 100%. Every truck has different equipment on-board so there are no standard figures to go by. But you can estimate your usage by doing research on specific gas powered appliances you plan to put into operation to help determine the tank size your truck will require.

Propane Tank Safety

To avoid potential problems with your propane tanks, keep the hoses that run from the tank to your truck secured. Do not leave hoses that are too long to sway freely with vehicle movement. The tanks on the outside of the vehicle need to be shielded from damage. Usually a steel cage can be placed around a tank. A leak indicator mounted inside the vehicle is also a great way to help prevent potentially dangerous incidents that can occur with these highly pressurized tanks.

A final note about propane tanks, they need to be securely mounted to your vehicle. These external propane tanks are also prone to damage in a vehicle accident and can cause dangerous situations on the streets. Protective covers may be required by local regulations before you can drive with on-board propane tanks. Many food truck owners mount their tanks on the rear of the vehicle while others can be mounted underneath. If mounting underneath, a saddle mount or horizontal mount tank will be required. Trailers

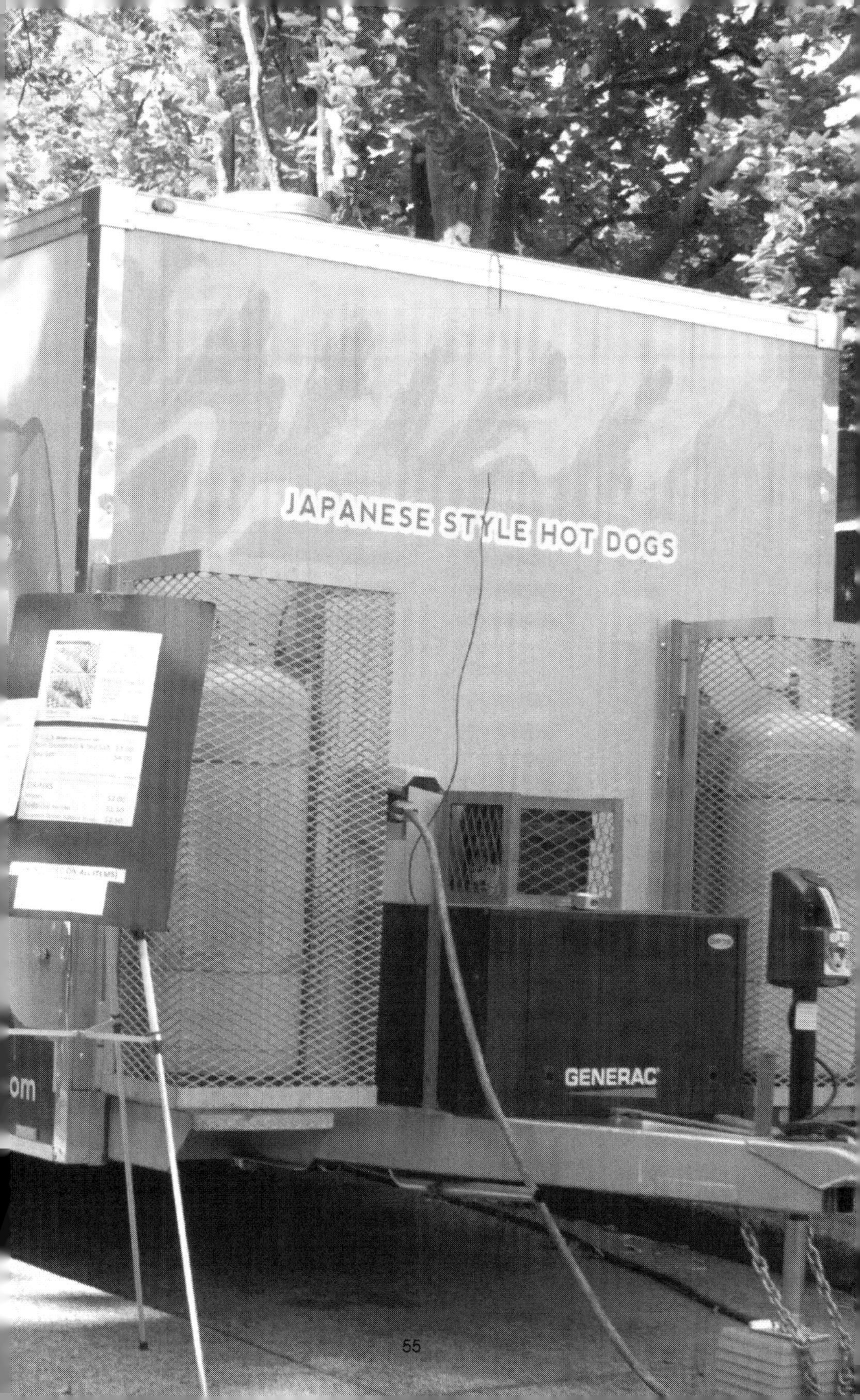
JAPANESE STYLE HOT DOGS
GENERAC

often have tanks secured on the trailer tongue that connects to a hitch.

Chapter 9: Plumbing and Water System

Another vital component of your food truck is the water system. At the heart of the water system is the built-in water tank. The water tanks in today's food trucks provide the same quality standards as those found in a restaurant sink. Water holding tanks have to be FDA approved in order for a food truck to pass inspection. There are strict requirements specifying that holding tanks must be constructed of strong materials and be easy to clean. Typical water tanks used in food trucks are made from polyethylene plaster resin which is non-corrosive. This is the same material that is used in kitchen tools like plastic bowls and other plastic utensils.

Water tanks that are seamless and constructed of one piece of plastic are the most effective at preventing leaks. It's also a good idea to consider a water tank that has UV protection to help avoid premature aging and cracking when exposed to sunlight. It's almost impossible to visually tell if the plastic water tank is brittle so the UV option can help prevent unexpected damage and prolong the life of your water system.

Fresh Water Tanks

Fresh water typically travels from the water tank to the faucets via an on-demand pump. This means that the pump only runs when the valve is open on your faucet. These pumps run on electricity so its wattage must be accounted for with the generator you are using. Some trucks and trailers have fresh water tanks mounted up high on a wall or ceiling allowing gravity to move water to your faucet. However, always check with your local health department to verify that you are installing your plumbing equipment to comply with codes.

As a responsible food truck owner, you must clean and sanitize water tanks on a regular basis to avoid contamination and foodborne illness. Because water tanks are meant to be used over a short period of time, they must be refilled regularly to help prevent problems related to standing water and bacteria growth.

Hot Water System

Hot running water is a necessity in any food service business. In a food truck, hot water must be generated inside the vehicle. Not only is it used for cooking, hot water is required for washing dirty utensils and cooking equipment. Water systems in food trucks use water heaters to produce hot water just like in homes or other businesses.

Water heaters that are used in food service vehicles are usually electrically powered. They are easy to install and efficient. They have reservoirs of varying capacities which could be an issue if you choose a water heater that is too small. There are also tank less models that generate hot water on demand. Tank less models are also powered by electricity but provide generous amounts of hot water as long as you have reserves in your fresh water tanks.

There are also water heaters that run on gas. This is great for reducing the load on your generator but it also introduces another issue. Gas water heaters need to be vented outside because of dangerous carbon monoxide fumes. A gas water heater requires a special enclosure to isolate fumes from the interior airspace of the truck. Gas water heaters can heat up water fast but may require additional attention by inspectors.

Sink Requirements

When it comes to sink requirements, food trucks must follow closely to the same standards that brick-and-mortar restaurants adhere to. Those basic policies require the installation of sinks with at least three compartments plus a hand-washing sink. The three compartment sinks are used for manually washing, rinsing and sanitizing the utensils, cooking equipment and tableware on-board your vehicle. Also, these sinks must be large to accommodate the biggest pieces of cooking equipment like pots and pans.

Properly designed sink systems have areas for rinsing and scraping food into garbage receptacles. After scraping left-over food off of utensils and other kitchen tools, items must be washed with detergent in the first sink compartment.

Water temperatures in the first compartment should be at least 110 degrees Fahrenheit. After prolonged use, the water and detergent must be replaced when suds are no longer present or the water appears dirty.

The second compartment is used for rinsing items after they've been washed. The water must be clean to remove all detergent and food particles when items are immersed.

The third compartment will sanitize the items that have been washed and rinsed. Hot water or chemical sanitizer can be used in this step. However, if plain hot water is to be used, it must be at least 171 degrees and items need to be submerged in the hot water for at least 30 seconds. Finally, all items that have been washed, rinsed and sanitized should be air dried on a clean drain board.

The hand washing sink is obviously for washing your hands and is smaller in size than the three compartment sinks. All food handlers are required to wash hands before touching or preparing any food. Frequent hand washing helps prevent cross-contamination when working with food.

Grey Water Tank

The water that you drain out of your sinks is called grey water and it must be stored on your vehicle until you can get to an approved disposal station. This water cannot legally be dumped in a storm or sewer drain. The grey water contains grease and food particles and must be disposed of properly. The facilities that accept grey water must have grease interceptors in place and be approved by the health department.

Grey water tanks need to be 15% larger than your fresh water tanks. That's because the waste water contains extra materials such as food waste which will take up more room in the tank. In addition, you may be dumping other liquids in your sinks like beverages and ice that will also drain into the grey water tanks. Most grey water tanks on food trucks and trailers are mounted underneath the vehicle (if there's space) so it doesn't take up additional room in the kitchen area. Others may mount these tanks under sinks inside the vehicle.

When building a food truck, take into consideration how much fresh water you will use before choosing a size. Sometimes truck builders will recommend fresh and grey water tanks that are much larger than you actually need. This not only increases your expenses but also the additional water contributes significant weight to your vehicle. Just for your reference, 1 gallon of water equals approximately 8 pounds. Typical sizes for water tanks in a single food service vehicle are:

30-35 gallon fresh water
50-55 gallon grey water

Though tank sizes can vary, your local city or county health department may have minimum size requirements specifically for your vehicle. Whether it's fresh water or grey water, you want to have an adequate supply and capacity so you don't run into issues during your service times.

Chapter 10: Venting and Fire Suppression

If you are cooking inside your vehicle, regulations require that you have a vent system. The vent system consists of two parts. The vent hood and the exhaust fan. Vent hoods are mounted over the cooking area such as a stove or griddle. In a food service vehicle, they are typically placed closer to the cooking surface than in a brick-and-mortar restaurant because of lower ceiling clearance. Hoods are often custom built to fit the exact width over the cooking area inside your vehicle. Custom truck builders can fabricate these units in their shops and install them as part of the food truck conversion process. Vent hoods are often made of stainless steel and integrated with a custom fabricated work surface where your cooking equipment will be mounted.

The second part of the venting system includes an exhaust fan mounted on the exterior of the vehicle... usually on the roof right above the vent hood. The cooking fumes are channeled out of the vehicle from ducting connected to the vent hood. Duct and exhaust fan sizes for your vehicle are determined by the type of cooking equipment that will be installed.

Running an exhaust fan usually requires a 120 volt electrical power source. So again take note of the wattage the fan needs in order to run. During your food service, cooking creates steam and vaporized grease which is sucked out of the vehicle by the exhaust fan. This airborne mixture can cause a mess. Over time, this exhaust can condense and create sludge. Because of this, exhaust fans have built-in grease cups to prevent excess grease from collecting and dripping onto your vehicle.

Exhaust systems must be regularly inspected for grease build-up to help prevent issues like fires. Inspections are typically required on a monthly basis for businesses that burn fuel like charcoal or wood burning ovens.

Fire Suppression Equipment

An integral part of food truck safety involves the fire suppression system built into the vehicle. Fire suppression equipment is required on all food service vehicles. Like brick-and-mortar restaurants, hot cooking surfaces, open flames, oils, chemicals and electrical connections all create a volatile situation that can cause small flames to quickly get out of control. Any fire in and around your vehicle can cause significant expense or bodily injury to those nearby. This can devastate your business and close you down for good.

An automatic fire suppression system is required before your truck can be put into operation. That's because about 60% of all restaurant fires involve hot cooking equipment. Automatic systems can suppress flames with chemicals and automatically shut down gas lines. The fire system can also shut off electricity which could further fuel the fire or cause additional dangers. While approval is needed before you go into operation, your fire suppression system is also required to have semi-annual inspections to verify that it will function correctly when needed.

As a further precaution, additional portable fire extinguishers may be required to help put out fires in other parts of the vehicle. There are two types of portable fire extinguishers used in food service establishments. Extinguishers with a Class K rating is intended for kitchen fires that involve grease and oils that burn at high temperatures. Class K fire extinguishers are meant to be used only after the automatic fire system has been activated.

Secondary Fire Extinguishers

A secondary fire extinguisher to keep on your vehicle is a Class ABC. This type of extinguisher is mainly used for non-grease fires from paper, plastics, wood and electrical sources. It's good policy to have a Class ABC extinguisher stored inside the cab of the vehicle as well as the kitchen area. Make sure all persons working in the vehicle know the location and operation of fire systems and extinguishers.

In the event of a fire, you should have an evacuation plan in place right from the launch of your business. Fire suppression systems can buy you time to escape your vehicle. But getting out as quickly as possible should be your first priority. In case of fire, call 911 and do not re-enter your vehicle until fire officials deem it safe.

Conclusion

The food truck industry has allowed many people to become first-time entrepreneurs. One of the attractive parts of starting a food truck business is that it is less costly than starting other types of businesses. But even with low startup costs, it isn't necessarily cheap. Your food truck will probably be the largest single expense you will incur when starting out. Knowing what types of trucks are available along with some general knowledge can help reduce stress and sticker shock when shopping for a vehicle.

A food truck consists of many systems that must work together seamlessly. Finding the right vehicle does not have to be complicated as long as you are aware of your requirements and what to look out for. Food trucks and vehicles that can be converted to a mobile kitchen are plentiful. Buying a previously owned food truck can be a money saver when you couple that with a reliable truck builder.

When selecting a custom truck builder, it is worth your time to research several companies and evaluate the type of work they have done in the past. Some of these builders may have truck inventory they can sell to customers but often, their customers will bring a vehicle to them for conversion.

A builder can complete many (if not all) phases in the construction of your truck. From concept to final delivery, a reputable food truck builder can really help you start out with a bang! There may be parts of the build that have to be outsourced to third-party vendors like graphic design, fire suppression equipment, certified electricians, propane installers and other regulated systems.

A builder is going to need a lot of input from you in order to bring life to your ideas. Even if your builder has completed hundreds of mobile kitchens before you, realize that each one is unique. Your input is vital to getting an end product that fits your needs. There should be no surprises when you take delivery of your vehicle. Of course you can do some of the construction work yourself but leave it to the experts to tackle the tough parts of your build.

Starting a food truck business allows you the freedom to dictate your own hours and the ability to exercise unlimited creativity. The food truck industry continues to grow and there's always room for new trucks on the road! Good luck on your journey!

Books Available in the
Food Truck Startup Series

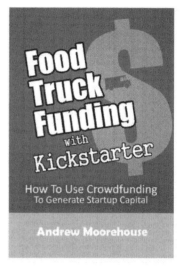

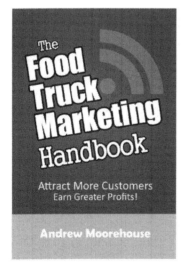

Made in the USA
Columbia, SC
02 February 2018